Top Tips For Starting A Successful YouTube

Contents

Introduction 8
   Testimonials 9
   Positive examples 10
      Tech Review Niche 10
      Sports Coverage Niche 12
      Gaming Niche..14
      News Reporting Niche 16
      Beauty Niche 18
   Negative examples..20
      Gamming Niche 20
      Tech Niche...22
      Fitness Niche 25
      DIY Niche 26
      Travel Niche 27
Tip 1 28
   Define Your Niche 28
      Understanding the Importance of a Niche.....................28
      Targeted Audience...28
   Insights 32
Tip 2 33
   Develop a Content Strategy..33
      Understanding Content Strategy 33
      Examples of Successful Content Strategies 37

- Insights 40
- Tip 3 41
  - Invest in Quality Equipment 41
    - Essential Equipment for YouTube Success 41
    - Additional Accessories 46
    - Budgeting for Your Equipment When starting: 47
  - Insights 48
- Tip 4 49
  - Create Engaging Thumbnails 49
    - Understanding the Importance of Thumbnails. 49
    - Best Practices for Designing Thumbnails 50
    - Tools for Creating Thumbnails 52
    - Examples of Effective Thumbnails 54
  - Insights 56
- Tip 5 57
  - Craft Compelling Titles and Descriptions 57
    - The Importance of Titles 57
    - Examples of Great Titles and Descriptions 61
  - Insights 63
- Tip 6 64
  - Master the Art of Editing 64
    - Understanding the Editing Process 64
    - Essential Editing Techniques 65
    - Tips for Efficient Editing 69
  - Insights 71
- Tip 7 72

- Optimize Your Video for Success 72
  - Understanding Video Optimization 72
  - Insights 78
- Tip 8 79
  - Build Your Community 79
    - Understanding the Importance of Community 79
    - Strategies for Building Your Community 80
    - Foster a Positive Environment 83
  - Insights 85
- Tip 9 86
  - Analyze Your Performance 86
  - Insights 92
- Tip 10 93
  - Monetization Strategies 93
    - Understanding YouTube Monetization 93
  - Insights 99
- Tip 11 100
  - Stay Consistent and Evolve 100
    - The Importance of Consistency 100
    - Strategies for Staying Consistent 101
  - Insight 105
- Tip 12 106
  - Navigating Challenges and Setbacks 106
    - Understanding Common Challenges 106
    - Strategies for Overcoming Challenges 108
    - Maintaining a Positive Mindset 111

- Insights 112
- Tip 13 113
  - Leveraging Trends and Collaboration 113
    - Understanding Trends 113
    - How to Identify Trends 114
    - Collaborating with Other Creators 115
    - Making the Most of Trends and Collaborations 119
  - Insights 120
- Tip 14 121
  - Building Your Brand Beyond 121
    - Understanding Personal Branding 121
    - Expanding Your Brand 122
    - Networking and Collaborations 125
    - Maintaining Your Brand Identity 126
  - Insights 127
- Tip 15 129
  - Analyzing Your Growth and Metrics 129
    - Understanding YouTube Analytics 129
    - Key Metrics to Monitor 130
    - Analyzing Your Growth 133
    - Making Informed Decisions 135
  - Insights 136
- Conclusion 137
  - Remember the key lessons 137
- Good Luck 139

Copyright © 2024 Andrew Remington

All rights reserved.

No part of this book is to be recreated or used elsewhere without the permission of the original publisher.

Introduction

Welcome to the dynamic world of YouTube, where creativity knows no bounds and anyone with a passion can find their voice. In a landscape brimming with diverse content, from heartwarming vlogs to informative tutorials, the opportunities for aspiring creators are endless. But with this vast potential comes the challenge of standing out in a sea of competition. How do you transform your unique ideas into a thriving channel that captivates audiences and keeps them coming back for more? This book is designed to guide you on your journey to becoming a successful YouTuber, whether you're a complete beginner or looking to refine your existing channel. We'll explore 15 essential tips that will empower you to define your niche, enhance your content, and engage with your audience in meaningful ways. Each chapter is packed with actionable insights and proven strategies to help you navigate the complexities of content creation and channel growth. As you dive into these pages, remember that every successful YouTuber started with a single idea and the courage to share it. Embrace your passion, harness your creativity, and let this guide serve as your roadmap to unlocking your full potential on YouTube. Get ready to embark on an exciting adventure that could transform your dreams into reality!

Testimonials

Welcome to an insightful exploration of the YouTube journey! In this collection, you will find a balanced mix of experiences from creators who have navigated the vibrant world of content creation.

You'll encounter five positive examples showcasing successful YouTube channels, where creators have thrived through dedication, strategic engagement, and creativity. These stories highlight the keys to their success and the valuable lessons they've learned along the way.

On the flip side, we will also share five negative examples from creators who faced challenges that hindered their growth. These testimonials delve into the common pitfalls and mistakes made, providing a candid look at what went wrong and the lessons learned from their experiences.

Whether you're an aspiring YouTuber or simply curious about the dynamics of content creation, these testimonials offer valuable insights into both the triumphs and tribulations of building a successful channel. Let's dive in!

Positive examples

Tech Review Niche

"When I first started my YouTube channel, Tech Savvy Reviews, I was just a tech enthusiast sharing my passion for gadgets and software. I remember sitting in my small apartment with my phone propped up on a stack of books, recording my first review of a budget smartphone. I had no idea what I was doing, but I was excited! Fast forward two years, and what started as a hobby has turned into a thriving channel with over 500,000 subscribers and millions of views. The journey has been incredible, but it wasn't always easy. I faced challenges like creative burnout, negative comments, and the pressure to keep up with rapid tech trends. What truly transformed my channel was understanding the importance of engagement. I made it a priority to respond to every comment and ask my viewers what they wanted to see next. This not only built a loyal community but also helped me create content that resonated with my audience. I learned that a simple 'thank you' or a thoughtful reply could turn casual viewers into passionate followers. Collaborating with other tech reviewers was another game-changer. When I teamed up with a fellow creator for a dual review of the latest gaming console, we introduced each other's audiences to our content. The cross-promotion skyrocketed both our channels! Analytics became my best friend, helping me identify which videos worked and which didn't. I remember when my 'Top 5 Budget Laptops for Students' video took off unexpectedly—I realized my audience craved value-focused content. From then on, I tailored my reviews to highlight affordability without compromising quality. Building my brand beyond YouTube was crucial too. I launched a website for in-depth reviews and started an Instagram account to share snippets and behind-the-scenes glimpses. This multi-platform approach broadened my reach and established my authority in the tech niche. Looking back, I can't believe how far I've come. What began as a small channel has turned into a full-time career. I've had the opportunity to attend tech expos, collaborate with major brands, and even launch my own line of tech accessories! To anyone thinking about starting a YouTube channel, I say: dive in! Embrace the journey, adapt to the challenges, and most importantly, engage with your audience. The tech industry moves fast, but with passion and perseverance, you can carve out your own niche and make a real impact. Remember, every expert was once a beginner, and your voice matters!"

Sports Coverage Niche

"When I launched my YouTube channel, Sports Spotlight, I was just a passionate sports fan with a dream of bringing unique coverage and analysis to fellow enthusiasts. I started with a simple setup—my phone and a makeshift tripod—filming my reactions to live games from my living room. I had no idea how much this journey would change my life! Fast forward three years, and I now have over 300,000 subscribers and a vibrant community of sports lovers who tune in for my game analyses, player interviews, and live commentary. The road wasn't always smooth; I faced challenges like dealing with negative comments, the pressure to keep up with constant sports news, and finding my unique voice in a crowded niche. One of the biggest turning points for my channel was realizing the power of engagement. I made it a mission to respond to as many comments as possible and to ask my viewers what they wanted to see next. This not only made my audience feel valued but also helped me tailor my content to what they were really interested in. For example, when I asked for feedback on which teams to cover more, I was thrilled to see my audience rally around their favorite underdog teams! Collaborating with other sports creators was another game-changer. When I partnered with a fellow YouTuber for a breakdown of the playoffs, we were able to bring our fans together, creating a buzz that neither of us could have achieved alone. It was amazing to see both channels grow from that collaboration! Analytics became my secret weapon, showing me exactly which videos resonated with my audience. I remember my video on "The Rise of Underdog Teams This Season" blew up, and I realized that my viewers loved stories of perseverance and grit. Since then, I've made it a point to highlight these narratives in my content. Expanding my brand beyond YouTube also played a crucial role. I started a podcast to dive deeper into sports discussions and launched an Instagram account for real-time game updates and fan interactions. This multi-platform approach helped me build a loyal following and solidify my reputation in the sports coverage niche. Looking back, I can hardly believe how far I've come. What started as a fun way to share my sports passion has turned into a fulfilling career. I've had the chance to cover live events, interview athletes, and even collaborate with major sports brands! To anyone considering starting a sports coverage channel, I say: go for it! Embrace the challenges, engage with your audience, and always stay true to your passion. The sports world is fast-paced and ever-changing, but with dedication and creativity, you can carve out your place and make a real impact. Remember, every sports fan has a voice—let yours be heard!"

Gaming Niche

"When I started my YouTube channel, I was just a casual gamer recording my gameplay and sharing my thoughts on the latest releases. Armed with a basic headset and a screen capture software, I dove into the world of gaming content creation, unsure of what to expect. Fast forward to today, and I'm thrilled to say that my channel has grown to over 400,000 subscribers, and I've turned my passion into a full-time career! The journey hasn't been without its ups and downs. I faced challenges like dealing with trolls in the comments section, the overwhelming pressure to keep up with new game releases and finding my unique style in a sea of gaming channels. But every setback became a stepping stone to success! One of the most impactful changes I made was actively engaging with my audience. I started responding to comments and asking viewers for their opinions on games and what content they'd like to see next. This not only fostered a community but also helped me tailor my videos to meet their interests. For instance, when I did a poll asking which game series to cover next, the response was overwhelming! I ended up diving deep into a fan-favorite franchise, and that video became one of my most-watched! Collaborating with other gaming YouTubers also played a huge role in my growth. I teamed up with fellow gamers for multiplayer gameplay and co-op challenges, which brought both our audiences together. It was a win-win situation—more fun and more exposure for everyone involved! Analytics became my trusty sidekick, guiding me through the labyrinth of content creation. By studying my audience retention and engagement metrics, I discovered that my "Let's Play" videos on indie games consistently performed well. I realized that my viewers loved discovering hidden gems, so I embraced that niche and began focusing more on indie game reviews and gameplay. Expanding my brand beyond YouTube was another key decision. I launched a Twitch channel for live streaming and started an Instagram account to share clips and gaming memes. This multi-platform approach not only broadened my reach but also allowed me to connect with my audience in real-time, creating a more personal experience. Looking back, I can hardly believe how far I've come. What started as a hobby has transformed into a thriving career, with opportunities to attend gaming expos, beta-test new releases, and collaborate with major game developers! To anyone thinking about starting a gaming channel, I say: just hit record! Embrace the chaos, build relationships with your audience, and always stay true to your gaming passion. The gaming community is vast and vibrant, and with creativity and dedication, you can carve out your own space and make a meaningful impact. Remember, every gamer has a story—let yours be told!"

News Reporting Niche

"When I launched my YouTube channel, I aimed to provide viewers with concise, engaging news updates that cut through the noise of traditional media. As a former journalist with a passion for storytelling, I wanted to deliver news that was not only informative but also relatable. Starting from my small apartment with a basic camera, I had a vision of creating a platform for meaningful discussions. Now, I'm proud to say that my channel has grown to over 500,000 subscribers! Several key factors contributed significantly to my success, I made it a priority to cover current events as they unfolded, ensuring that my content was timely and relevant. By staying on top of breaking news and providing updates on ongoing stories, I attracted viewers looking for the latest information. I often posted videos within hours of major events, which helped establish my channel as a go-to source for timely news. I developed a format that presented news stories in a clear and concise manner. My videos typically ranged from 5 to 10 minutes, focusing on the most important details without overwhelming viewers with excessive information. This format resonated with busy audiences who appreciated the straightforward delivery of news. I utilized storytelling techniques to make news reports more engaging. By framing stories with a human touch—sharing personal anecdotes, interviews, or community reactions—I brought a relatable angle to the news that helped viewers connect emotionally with the topics being discussed. I encouraged viewers to share their thoughts and opinions in the comments section and often featured viewer responses in my videos. This interaction fostered a sense of community and made my audience feel valued and involved in the discussion. I actively promoted my content on social media platforms, sharing video clips and highlights to attract a wider audience. By engaging with followers on platforms like Twitter and Instagram, I drove traffic to my YouTube channel and created a multi-platform presence that strengthened my brand. Reflecting on my journey, I've learned that timeliness, concise presentation, engaging storytelling, community building, and effective promotion are essential for success in the news reporting niche. To aspiring news creators, I encourage you to stay passionate about your subjects, connect with your audience, and continuously adapt to the ever-changing landscape of news media!"

Beauty Niche

"When I embarked on my YouTube journey, I was a young makeup enthusiast with a dream of sharing my passion for beauty and self-expression. I started filming from my small bedroom, using my phone to capture makeup tutorials and skincare tips. Fast forward to now, and I'm thrilled to have built a community of over 800,000 subscribers who share my love for all things beauty! I made it a priority to be authentic and relatable in my videos. I shared not only my makeup skills but also my personal experiences, including my struggles with skin issues and self-confidence. This vulnerability resonated with viewers, making them feel connected to me and my journey. I invested in better equipment, including a high-quality camera and lighting setup. I also learned video editing techniques that enhanced the overall production value of my content. High-quality visuals and audio significantly improved viewer engagement and made my videos more enjoyable to watch. I actively engaged with my audience through comments, social media, and live Q&A sessions. I made it a point to respond to viewer questions and suggestions, which fostered a sense of community and loyalty. I often asked for their input on what types of videos they wanted to see, and that feedback shaped much of my content. I partnered with established YouTubers for makeup challenges and tutorials, which introduced my channel to new audiences. These collaborations not only expanded my reach but also strengthened my connections within the beauty community. By creating timely content around popular products or viral challenges, I was able to attract viewers looking for the latest beauty insights. Staying relevant in the fast-paced beauty world helped maintain my channel's growth. Looking back on my journey, I've learned that authenticity, quality production, audience engagement, collaboration, and trend awareness are essential for success in the beauty niche. To aspiring beauty creators, I encourage you to embrace your uniqueness, connect with your audience, and never stop learning and evolving in your craft!"

Negative examples

Gamming Niche

"When I first launched my YouTube channel, I was brimming with excitement and ideas. I envisioned it as a fun space to share my gameplay, review the latest releases, and connect with fellow gamers. Armed with an entry-level camera and a passion for gaming, I dove headfirst into content creation. Fast forward 18 months, and my channel is a ghost town with just 2,000 subscribers and a handful of views. Looking back, one of my biggest mistakes was a lack of consistency. I started with a bang, posting videos almost daily, but soon burned out. I went from daily uploads to sporadic posts, which left my audience confused and disengaged. YouTube thrives on consistency, and I failed to establish a reliable schedule that would keep viewers coming back for more. Another major misstep was not understanding my niche. I tried to cover everything from mobile games to high-end PC titles without honing in on a specific audience. This scattered approach made it difficult for viewers to know what to expect. I should have focused on a particular genre or type of content, whether it was indie games, horror games, or live streams, to build a dedicated following. Engagement was another area where I fell short. I posted videos but didn't actively interact with my audience. I rarely replied to comments or asked for feedback, which made viewers feel like they were just another number on my analytics dashboard. Building a community is crucial, and I neglected to foster that connection, ultimately leading to viewer apathy. I also underestimated the power of branding. My channel lacked a clear identity—my thumbnails were inconsistent, and my channel art was thrown together in a hurry. A strong brand helps creators stand out, and without it, I blended into the background of the vast YouTube landscape. I should have invested time in developing a cohesive aesthetic that represented my content and personality. Finally, I didn't take the time to analyze my metrics. I posted videos but rarely checked my analytics to understand what worked and what didn't. Had I looked at my audience retention rates, I might have realized that my longer videos were losing viewers quickly. I could have adapted my content based on viewer preferences, which might have improved engagement and growth. Now, as I step away from YouTube, I've gained invaluable lessons from this experience. While it's disappointing to see my channel not succeed as I hoped, I've learned the importance of consistency, knowing your niche, engaging with your audience, building a strong brand, and analyzing performance metrics. To anyone starting a channel, I say: plan carefully and be prepared for the long haul. Don't rush into content creation without a strategy. Focus on building a community, stay true to your niche, and don't underestimate the power of branding and engagement. Each failure is a stepping stone to success—just make sure you learn from it!"

Tech Niche

"When I launched my YouTube channel, I was fueled by my passion for technology and a desire to share my insights on the latest gadgets and software. I envisioned a channel where I could provide in-depth reviews, tutorials, and tech news. Armed with a decent camera and editing software, I set out to create engaging content. Fast forward two years, and I found myself with only 1,500 subscribers and dwindling views. It's time to unpack what went wrong and the lessons learned from this experience. One of my first mistakes was not defining a clear niche for my channel. Tech is a vast field, and I tried to cover everything from smartphone reviews to computer hardware to software tutorials. This lack of focus confused my audience. One week I'd post about the latest smartphone, and the next, I'd pivot to a deep dive into gaming PCs. Viewers didn't know what to expect, making it difficult to build a loyal subscriber base. I realized that honing in on a specific niche—whether it's mobile tech, gaming, or software development—could have attracted a more dedicated audience interested in that particular area. A focused approach would have helped me establish authority and credibility in a specific domain. I was enthusiastic and uploaded videos almost daily. However, as time went on, I struggled to maintain that pace. I went from daily uploads to posting once every few weeks. This inconsistency hurt my channel's growth; my audience didn't know when to expect new content, leading to disengagement. Establishing a regular upload schedule is crucial for retention. I should have aimed for quality over quantity, focusing on a consistent schedule that balanced my capacity to create high-quality content and my audience's expectations. I posted videos but failed to interact meaningfully with my audience. I rarely responded to comments or asked for feedback on what they wanted to see next. As a result, my viewers felt disconnected from the channel, and I missed out on valuable insights into their preferences. Engaging with my audience is essential for building a community. I should have responded to comments, asked questions, and even created polls to involve viewers in the content creation process. Building relationships with my audience would have fostered loyalty and encouraged more interaction on my videos. My channel lacked a cohesive identity—my thumbnails were made quickly, my channel art was boring, and my intros and outros were weak. Without strong branding, I struggled to stand out in a crowded niche. I learned that investing time in creating a strong brand identity is crucial. A professional logo, consistent thumbnail style, and cohesive visuals help communicate the channel's personality and attract viewers. A polished presentation can make a significant difference in first impressions, I rarely thought of my YouTube analytics. I didn't analyze which videos performed well or where viewers dropped off. If I had taken the time to review my analytics, I would have noticed trends that could inform my content strategy. I often stuck to my planned content schedule without considering current events or emerging technologies. For instance, when a groundbreaking gadget was released, I missed the opportunity to capitalize on it by not pivoting my content to address the buzz. I learned that timely content can attract new viewers looking for information on popular topics, so I should have been more agile in my approach. I learned that the road to success on YouTube is filled with challenges and lessons. While it's disheartening to see my channel not thrive as I hoped, I've gained invaluable insights that I'll carry into future endeavors. To anyone considering starting a YouTube channel, my advice is to define your niche, maintain consistency, engage with your audience, invest in branding, analyze your performance, and stay adaptable to trends. Each misstep is an opportunity for growth, so embrace them as part of the process. Remember, the world of content creation is ever-evolving, and by learning from your experiences, you can rise again, stronger and more equipped for success!"

Fitness Niche

"When I started my YouTube channel, I was passionate about health and fitness, eager to share my workout routines and nutrition tips. I envisioned a community of fitness enthusiasts who would be inspired by my journey. With a decent camera and a background in personal training, I jumped into content creation. However, two years later, my channel stagnated at just 900 subscribers, and I found myself disheartened. However, as I juggled work and personal life, my uploads became sporadic. I went from consistent weekly videos to posting once a month. My audience didn't know when to expect new content, leading to a significant drop in engagement. I should have prioritized consistency over frequency, ensuring my audience had reliable content to look forward to. I tried to cover everything from HIIT workouts to yoga and nutrition advice. This scattered approach confused viewers about what to expect from my channel, making it difficult to build a dedicated audience. Focusing on a specific niche—like bodyweight workouts for busy professionals—could have helped me attract a more targeted audience interested in that particular area. I didn't ask for feedback or respond to comments, which left my audience feeling disconnected. I should have solicited feedback and responded to comments to foster loyalty and connection. In retrospect, the experience taught me valuable lessons about consistency, niche focus, and audience engagement. My advice to aspiring creators is to plan carefully and prioritize building relationships with your audience. Each misstep is a stepping stone to improvement!"

DIY Niche

"When I launched my YouTube channel, I was filled with enthusiasm for crafting and home improvement projects. I wanted to share my love for creativity with others, showcasing everything from simple crafts to elaborate home renovations. Armed with a basic camera, I set off on my journey. However, after a year, I found myself with only 1,000 subscribers and limited engagement. It's time to share what went wrong. While I had great ideas, my video quality didn't match my vision. I filmed with poor lighting and didn't pay attention to audio quality, which made it hard for viewers to engage with my content. Investing in good lighting and audio equipment can significantly enhance the viewing experience. Quality matters, especially in a visually-driven niche like DIY. I tried various styles—from quick tutorials to lengthy project walkthroughs—without a clear direction. This inconsistency made it difficult for viewers to know what to expect, leading to confusion. Developing a consistent style and format helps viewers identify with the channel. I should have focused on a specific type of content, such as quick, easy DIY projects for beginners. I relied solely on YouTube's algorithm to promote my videos and didn't actively share my content on social media or collaborate with other creators. This lack of promotion limited my reach and audience growth. Actively promoting content on social media and collaborating with others in the niche can expand reach and attract new viewers. Building a network is essential for growth. Reflecting on my time, I learned the importance of video quality, consistency, and proactive promotion."

Travel Niche

"When I started on my YouTube journey, I was eager to share my travel adventures and tips with the world. With a passion for exploring new places, I envisioned a channel filled with engaging travel vlogs and destination guides. Armed with a camera and a spirit of adventure, I set off. However, after a year, my channel plateaued at only 5000 subscribers. I traveled to various locations and created vlogs for each, but without a consistent theme or focus. One week I'd cover a beach destination, and the next, a city tour. This inconsistency made it hard for viewers to connect with my channel. Defining a consistent theme—like budget travel or adventure travel—could have helped attract a dedicated audience interested in that type of content. While my videos featured beautiful locations, I often neglected storytelling. I didn't craft engaging narratives or share personal experiences, leaving viewers feeling detached. Incorporating storytelling into travel vlogs enhances viewer engagement. Sharing personal experiences and insights can make the content more relatable and enjoyable. I didn't pay attention to SEO and often used vague titles and descriptions. As a result, my videos struggled to gain visibility in search results. Understanding SEO best practices—using relevant keywords and crafting engaging titles—can significantly improve video discoverability. Investing time in optimizing content can lead to greater exposure. I learned valuable lessons about theme consistency, storytelling, and the importance of SEO. To aspiring creators, I recommend focusing on a clear theme, engaging storytelling, and optimizing your content for search."

Tip 1

Define Your Niche

Defining your niche is one of the most critical steps in launching a successful YouTube channel. Your niche is the specific topic or area of interest that your channel will focus on, and it plays a pivotal role in attracting a dedicated audience. In this chapter, we'll explore how to identify your niche, understand its significance, and ensure it aligns with your passion and expertise.

Understanding the Importance of a Niche

Targeted Audience

A well-defined niche allows you to target a specific audience, making it easier to attract viewers who are genuinely interested in your content. This targeted approach fosters community engagement and loyalty, as viewers are more likely to return for content that resonates with their interests.

Reduced Competition

While YouTube is saturated with content, focusing on a specific niche can help you stand out. Instead of competing with millions of general creators, you can carve out a space for yourself in a less crowded area, where your unique perspective adds value.

Brand Identity

Your niche helps establish your brand identity. It shapes your content style, tone, and messaging, making it easier for viewers to understand what to expect from your channel. A strong brand identity can lead to better recognition and recall.

Steps to Identify Your Niche

Reflect on Your Passions and Interests: Start by listing topics you are passionate about or have expertise in. Consider what excites you, what you love discussing, and what you could talk about endlessly. Your enthusiasm will translate into your content, making it more engaging for viewers.

Research Audience Needs:

Once you have a list of potential niches, research audience needs and interests within those topics. Use tools like Google Trends, YouTube search suggestions, and social media platforms to gauge what people are searching for or discussing. This research will help you identify gaps in the market where your content can provide value.

Analyze Competitors:

Look at existing channels within your potential niches. Analyze their content, subscriber counts, and viewer engagement. Identify what they do well and where they might fall short. This competitive analysis will inform your strategy and help you find unique angles to approach your content.

Experiment and Adapt:

Don't be afraid to experiment with different types of content when starting. Create a few videos across your chosen niche to see what resonates with your audience. Pay attention to viewer feedback and analytics; this data can guide you in refining your niche and content strategy.

Consider Long-Term Sustainability:

While it's essential to choose a niche that excites you, also consider its long-term sustainability. Ensure that the topic has enough depth and breadth for you to create content consistently over time. A niche that evolves with trends or allows for sub-topics can provide ongoing inspiration. Build your niche around your values once you've identified your niche, it's crucial to align it with your values and mission.

Consider the following

Authenticity

Be true to yourself and your values. Authenticity resonates with audiences, and viewers are more likely to connect with a creator who is genuine. Share your personal experiences and perspectives to build trust.

Impact

Think about the impact you want your channel to have on your audience. Whether it's educating, entertaining, inspiring, or motivating, having a clear mission can guide your content creation and strengthen your connection with viewers.

Community Engagement

Foster a sense of community within your niche. Engage with your audience through comments, social media, and live streams. Encouraging discussions and feedback will not only enhance viewer loyalty but also provide valuable insights into content preferences.

Insights

Defining your niche is a foundational step in your YouTube journey. It shapes your brand, influences your content strategy, and connects you with your audience. By reflecting on your passions, researching audience needs, analyzing competitors, and aligning your niche with your values, you can carve out a unique space in the YouTube ecosystem. Embrace this opportunity to express yourself and share your knowledge with the world and remember that the journey is just as important as the destination. With a clear niche, you're well on your way to creating compelling content that resonates with viewers and fosters a thriving community.

Tip 2

Develop a Content Strategy

A well-thought-out content strategy is essential for the success of your YouTube channel. It serves as the backbone of your video creation process, guiding you on what to produce, how often to post, and how to engage with your audience. In this chapter, we will explore the components of a successful content strategy, including types of content, planning, and consistency, along with practical examples to help you get started.

Understanding Content Strategy

Content Types

The first step in developing your content strategy is to identify the types of content you want to create. There are various formats you can explore, including:

Vlogs
Personal insights and experiences (e.g., travel vlogs, daily life).

Tutorials

Step-by-step guides on specific skills (e.g., cooking, DIY projects).

Reviews

Assessments of products or services (e.g., tech gadgets, books).

Challenges

Fun or engaging challenges that involve your audience (e.g., 30-day challenges).

Interviews

Conversations with experts or influencers in your niche.

Content Themes

Within your chosen content types, establish recurring themes that align with your niche. For instance, if your niche is fitness, your themes could include workout routines, nutrition tips, and wellness challenges.

Planning Your Content

Create a Content Calendar

A content calendar helps you organize your video ideas, production timelines, and posting schedules. It ensures that you remain consistent and allows you to plan for seasonal or trending topics.

** Example **

Monthly Themes: Dedicate each month to a specific theme (e.g., January for fitness goals, February for healthy recipes).

Weekly Schedule: Plan to upload every Tuesday and Thursday, with different content types on each day (e.g., tutorials on Tuesday, vlogs on Thursday).

Brainstorm Video Ideas

Set aside time to brainstorm video ideas related to your themes. Use mind mapping or lists to generate a variety of concepts.

Example

if your niche is personal finance, your ideas might include: - "How to Create a Budget in 5 Simple Steps"

"Top 10 Apps for Tracking Your Expenses"

"My Journey to Paying Off Student Loans: Tips and Tricks"

Outline Your Videos

Before filming, create an outline for each video to ensure you cover key points and maintain a logical flow. This will help you stay organized and focused during production.

Consistency and Scheduling

Set a Posting Schedule: Consistency is vital for audience retention. Choose a posting frequency that works for you—whether it's once a week, bi-weekly, or monthly. Stick to your schedule to build viewer expectations. For example: If you decide to post weekly, notify your audience about your schedule (e.g., every Monday at 5 PM).

Batch Production

If possible, consider batching your video production. This involves filming multiple videos in one session, which allows you to stay ahead of your schedule and reduces the stress of last-minute content creation.

Engage with Your Audience

Encourage viewers to subscribe, like, and comment on your videos. Respond to comments and ask for feedback on future content. This interaction fosters a sense of community and helps you understand what your audience enjoys.

Examples of Successful Content Strategies

Fitness Channel

A fitness YouTuber might create a content strategy that includes:

Weekly Workout Videos: Uploading a new workout routine every Monday.

Monthly Challenges

Starting a 30-day fitness challenge every month, encouraging viewers to join and share their progress.

Nutrition Tips

Posting a "What I Eat in a Day" video every Thursday to complement workout routines.

Cooking Channel

A cooking enthusiast could establish a content strategy featuring:

Themed Cooking Series

Each month focusing on a different cuisine (e.g., Italian month, vegan month).

Seasonal Recipes

Creating videos around holidays or seasonal ingredients (e.g., summer BBQ recipes or winter comfort foods).

Live Cooking Sessions

Hosting monthly live streams where viewers can cook along and ask questions in real-time.

Tech Review Channel

A tech reviewer might employ a strategy that includes:

Weekly Reviews:

Posting in-depth reviews of the latest gadgets every Friday.

Comparison Videos:

Creating comparison videos between similar products (e.g., "iPhone vs. Samsung Galaxy").

Tech News Recaps:

Offering bi-weekly updates on the latest tech trends and news.

Insights

Developing a content strategy is essential for ensuring that your YouTube channel remains organized, engaging, and consistent. By identifying the types of content, you want to create, planning ahead with a content calendar, and maintaining a consistent posting schedule, you lay the groundwork for a successful channel. Use the examples provided to inspire your own strategy and remember that flexibility is key—don't hesitate to adapt your approach as you learn what resonates most with your audience. With a solid content strategy in place, you're one step closer to building a thriving YouTube community.

Tip 3
Invest in Quality Equipment

Investing in quality equipment is crucial for producing high-quality content that attracts and retains viewers. While it's possible to start with basic gear, upgrading to better equipment can significantly enhance your video and audio quality, making your content more professional and enjoyable to watch. We'll explore the essential equipment you need, provide recommendations, and suggest where to purchase these items.

Essential Equipment for YouTube Success

Camera

A good camera is vital for capturing high-quality video. While smartphones can work for beginners, investing in a dedicated camera can elevate your production quality.

Recommendations:

Entry-Level

Canon EOS M50 or Sony ZV-1 are great for beginners, offering excellent video quality and user-friendly features.

Mid-Range

Panasonic Lumix GH5 or Sony A6400 for more advanced features and better low-light performance.

Where to Buy:

You can purchase cameras from major retailers like Amazon, Best Buy, B&H Photo, or directly from the manufacturer's website.

Microphone

Clear audio is just as important as video quality. Viewers are more likely to click away from videos with poor sound.

Recommendations:

Lavalier Microphone: Rode Wireless GO II for on-the-go shooting and interviews.

-USB Microphone: Blue Yeti or Audio-Technica ATR2100x for stationary setups, perfect for voiceovers and commentary.

Where to Buy:

Check out Amazon, Sweetwater, or local music stores for a variety of microphone options.

Lighting

Proper lighting can transform your videos, making them look more professional. Good lighting helps reduce shadows and enhances overall video quality.

Recommendation:

Softbox Lights: Neewer Softbox Lighting Kit for diffused, even lighting.

Ring Light: Neewer Ring Light Kit for a flattering glow, ideal for beauty or talking-head videos.

Where to Buy:

Look for lighting kits on Amazon, eBay, or photography specialty stores.

Tripod/Stabilizer

A stable camera is essential to avoid shaky footage. A tripod allows for steady shots, while a stabilizer helps when moving around.

Recommendations:

Tripod: Manfrotto Compact Action Tripod for versatility and portability.

Gimbal Stabilizer: DJI Ronin-S for smooth, dynamic shots if you're shooting while moving.

Where to Buy:

You can find tripods and stabilizers on Amazon, B&H Photo, or local electronics stores.

Editing Software

Quality editing software allows you to enhance your videos, add effects, and create a polished final product.

Recommendations:

Beginner-Friendly: iMovie (Mac) or DaVinci Resolve (Windows/Mac) for free options.

Professional: Adobe Premiere Pro or Final Cut Pro for more advanced editing capabilities.

Where to Buy:

Editing software can be purchased directly from the software's website or through subscription services like Adobe Creative Cloud.

Additional Accessories

External Hard Drive

For storing footage, consider purchasing an external hard drive like the Seagate Expansion or Western Digital My Passport.

Green Screen

If you plan to use background effects, a collapsible green screen can be useful. Look for options from Neewer or Elgato.

Where to Buy:

These accessories can typically be found on Amazon, Best Buy, or specialized computer and photography stores.

Budgeting for Your Equipment When starting:

it's essential to strike a balance between quality and budget. Here are some tips on budgeting for your equipment:

Prioritize:

Determine which equipment is most crucial for your content. If you're focusing on vlogs, prioritize a good camera and microphone. For tutorials, invest in lighting first.

Buy Used:

Consider purchasing used or refurbished equipment to save money. Websites like B&H Photo, KEH, and eBay often have great deals on quality gear.

Start Small:

You don't need to buy everything at once. Start with the essentials and gradually upgrade your equipment as your channel grows.

Insights

Investing in quality equipment is a significant step toward creating professional-looking and sounding content. By carefully selecting the right camera, microphone, lighting, and accessories, you can enhance the overall quality of your videos and stand out in a crowded space. Remember, while equipment plays a vital role, your creativity and storytelling will ultimately define your channel. As you grow, continue to assess your equipment needs and make adjustments accordingly. With the right tools in hand, you're well on your way to producing engaging content that resonates with your audience.

Tip 4

Create Engaging Thumbnails

In the crowded world of YouTube, first impressions matter. Thumbnails are the first thing viewers see when browsing through videos, and an engaging thumbnail can significantly impact your click-through rate (CTR). In this chapter, we will discuss the importance of thumbnails, best practices for designing them, and tools you can use to create eye-catching visuals that entice viewers to click on your videos.

Understanding the Importance of Thumbnails.

First Impressions

Thumbnails serve as the cover art for your videos. A well-designed thumbnail can capture the attention of potential viewers and spark their curiosity. Conversely, a bland or unappealing thumbnail may cause viewers to scroll past your content.

Brand Recognition

Consistent thumbnail design helps build your brand identity. Using similar colors, fonts, and styles across your thumbnails allows viewers to recognize your content at a glance, fostering familiarity and trust.

Increased Click-Through Rate

Compelling thumbnails can lead to higher CTR, meaning more people are likely to click on your video. This can result in increased views, audience retention, and improved rankings in YouTube search results.

Best Practices for Designing Thumbnails

Use High-Quality Images

Always use high-resolution images that are clear and visually appealing. Blurry or pixelated images can create a negative impression and deter viewers.

Incorporate Text

Adding text to your thumbnails can help convey the essence of your video. Use bold, readable fonts and keep the text brief (ideally 3-5 words). Make sure the text contrasts well with the background for maximum visibility.

Choose Vibrant Colors

Bright and contrasting colors can make your thumbnail stand out among others. Use colors that reflect your brand identity, but ensure they draw attention without overwhelming the viewer.

Include Faces

Thumbnails featuring expressive faces tend to perform better. Human emotions can engage viewers and create a connection. If applicable, include close-up shots of yourself or other individuals featured in the video.

Maintain Consistency

Develop a consistent design style that reflects your brand. Use similar color schemes, fonts, and layouts across all your thumbnails to create a cohesive look for your channel.

Test Different Designs

Don't hesitate to experiment with different thumbnail designs and analyze their performance. Use YouTube Analytics to see which thumbnails generate higher CTR and adjust your approach accordingly.

Tools for Creating Thumbnails

Canva

A user-friendly graphic design platform that offers a variety of customizable templates specifically for YouTube thumbnails. You can easily drag and drop elements, add text, and apply filters.

-Website:

[Canva](https://www.canva.com)

Adobe Spark

Another excellent option for creating stunning thumbnails, Adobe Spark provides templates, design tools, and a simple interface that allows for quick customization.

Website:

[Adobe Spark](https://spark.adobe.com)

Photoshop

For those with more advanced graphic design skills, Adobe Photoshop offers extensive features for creating professional-quality thumbnails. You can manipulate images, create custom graphics, and refine your design to perfection.

Website:
[AdobePhotoshop](https://www.adobe.com/products/photoshop.html)

Fotor

A free online photo editing tool that includes templates and design features specifically for YouTube thumbnails. It's suitable for users who want a straightforward tool without advancedskills.

Website:

[Fotor] (https://www.fotor.com)

Snappa

Another graphic design tool that offers pre-made templates for YouTube thumbnails, making it easy to create visuals quickly and efficiently.

Website:

[Snappa] (https://snappa.com)

Examples of Effective Thumbnails

For a cooking channel, a thumbnail might feature a close-up of a delicious dish with bold text overlaying it, such as "5-Minute Pasta!" This showcases the end result and piques interest.

Vlogs

A travel vlogger might use a thumbnail with a vibrant landscape backdrop, showing the creator's excited expression with the text "Epic Adventure in Bali!" This conveys a sense of adventure while inviting viewers to join the journey.

Product Reviews

For a tech review channel, a thumbnail could display the product being reviewed alongside the text "Is It Worth It?" This directly addresses viewer curiosity and encourages clicks.

Insights

Creating engaging thumbnails is essential for attracting viewers to your videos. By following best practices—such as using high-quality images, incorporating text, choosing vibrant colors, and maintaining consistency—you can craft thumbnails that not only capture attention but also reflect your brand identity. Utilize the recommended tools to bring your thumbnail designs to life, and don't forget to test different styles to see what resonates best with your audience. With captivating thumbnails, you'll increase your chances of standing out in the competitive YouTube landscape and drawing viewers to your content.

Tip 5

Craft Compelling Titles and Descriptions

Welcome to the world of YouTube titles and descriptions, where creativity meets strategy. Just like a great book needs an enticing cover, your video needs a title and description that grab attention and inform viewers about what to expect. In this chapter, we'll explore the art of crafting compelling titles and descriptions that make viewers say, "I need to click on this!"—and not just because they're procrastinating from doing laundry.

The Importance of Titles

First Impressions Matter

Your title is often the first thing viewers see, and it's their first opportunity to judge whether your video is worth their precious time—or if they should stick with binge-watching cat videos instead. A good title can make the difference between a click and a scroll.

SEO Magic

Titles are also vital for search engine optimization (SEO). By including relevant keywords, you increase the chances of your video appearing in search results. It's like putting a neon sign on the side of the road that says, "Hey! Over here! This video is exactly what you're looking for!"

Create Curiosity

A well-crafted title should pique interest without giving everything away. Think of it as a movie trailer—enough excitement to get people to buy a ticket (or in this case, click on your video), but not so much that they feel like they've already seen the whole film.

Tips for Crafting Effective Titles

Keep It Short and Sweet:

Aim for titles that are concise and to the point. Ideally, keep them under 60 characters so they don't get cut off in search results. Remember, "How to Bake a Perfect Cake" is far more enticing than "A Detailed Explanation of the Intricacies Involved in Baking a Perfect Cake." Unless, of course, your audience is comprised of pastry chefs with a penchant for verbosity.

Use Numbers:

Titles that include numbers often stand out and imply a clear structure. For example, "5 Tips for a Flawless Skin Routine" sounds more manageable than "Tips for a Flawless Skin Routine," which could lead to an endless philosophical debate about what 'flawless' really means.

Ask Questions:

Titles that pose a question can engage viewers. "How Can You Save Money on Groceries?" invites curiosity and gives viewers a reason to find out what you have to say—because, let's be real, who doesn't want to save a few bucks?

Be Descriptive:

Make sure your title accurately reflects the content of your video. Misleading titles may get you clicks, but they'll also earn you an audience full of disappointed viewers who thought they were signing up for a cooking tutorial but got a 30-minute rant about the existential crisis of socks disappearing in the laundry.

The Role of Descriptions

Provide Context:

Your description offers an opportunity to expand on your title. Use it to provide context about the video, share what viewers can expect, and encourage them to take action (like subscribing or watching another video). Think of it as the movie synopsis that gives just enough away without spoiling the ending.

Include Keywords:

Just like your title, your description should include relevant keywords to improve SEO. This helps your video show up when people search for specific topics. For example, if your video is about "Easy Vegan Recipes," sprinkle that phrase throughout your description like confetti at a party.

Add Links and Calls to Action:

Use your description to link to your social media, website, or other videos. A well-placed call to action, such as "Don't forget to subscribe for more delicious content!" can gently nudge viewers toward engaging with your channel. Just don't be too pushy—think of it as an invitation to a party, not a hostage negotiation.

Examples of Great Titles and Descriptions

Title

"10 Life Hacks You Wish You Knew Sooner!"

Description:

"Ever feel like life could be a little easier? In this video, I share 10 genius life hacks that will save you time, money, and a whole lot of frustration. From kitchen tips to organization tricks, you won't want to miss these! Don't forget to subscribe for more hacks!"

Title:

"The Ultimate Guide to Plant Care: Keep Your Green Friends Alive!"

Description:

"Are your houseplants staging a rebellion? Fear not! This ultimate guide covers everything you need to know about keeping your green friends thriving. From watering woes to sunlight secrets, we've got you covered. Plus, subscribe for plant tips that even your cactus will appreciate!"

Title:

"Why You Should Stop Using Your Phone Before Bed (And What to Do Instead)"

Description:

"Are you struggling to fall asleep while scrolling through social media? In this video, we dive into the reasons why ditching your phone at bedtime could be the key to better sleep. Plus, we'll share some relaxing alternatives to help you unwind. Subscribe for more tips on living your best life!"

Insights

Crafting compelling titles and descriptions is essential for attracting viewers and improving your video's visibility on YouTube. By keeping titles short, using numbers and questions, and ensuring they reflect your content, you can create engaging hooks that entice viewers to click. Meanwhile, your descriptions should provide valuable context, include keywords, and guide viewers toward further engagement. With a little creativity and a sprinkle of humor, you can make your titles and descriptions stand out in a sea of content, ensuring that your videos don't just get watched—they get clicked!

Tip 6

Master the Art of Editing

Editing is where the magic happens! It transforms your raw footage into a polished final product, allowing you to showcase your creativity and storytelling skills. In this chapter, we'll explore the essentials of video editing, tips to make your edits shine, and how to avoid the common pitfall of "just one more cut" syndrome—because let's face it, sometimes less is more!

Understanding the Editing Process

Why Edit?

Editing is crucial for enhancing the quality of your videos. It allows you to remove mistakes, add effects, and create a smooth flow. Think of it as giving your video a makeover—a little trim here, a splash of color there, and voilà, it's ready for the red carpet!

Choosing an Editing Software

A good editing software is your best friend. Depending on your skill level and budget, here are some options:

Beginner-Friendly:

iMovie (Mac) or Windows Movie Maker (Windows) are great starting points for newbies who want to dip their toes into the editing pool without splashing too much.

Intermediate to Advanced:

Adobe Premiere Pro or Final Cut Pro offer more robust features for those ready to dive deeper. Just remember, with great power comes great responsibility—and a lot of buttons to click.

Essential Editing Techniques

Cutting and Trimming

The first step is to cut out any unnecessary footage. Be ruthless! If a scene doesn't add value or make you laugh, it's time to say goodbye. Imagine your video as a delicious cake: if a slice is burnt, just don't serve it. No one wants to risk a trip to the dentist!

Example

If you're making a tutorial video about how to bake cookies, you might have filmed a lengthy segment of you mixing the dough. If it's too long or includes moments where you're just staring blankly at the ingredients, trim it down to the essentials. Keep only the parts where you explain the steps clearly or add a funny quip about the time you forgot to add sugar (because who hasn't been there?).

Transitions

Smooth transitions can enhance the flow of your video. Use simple cuts, fades, or wipes to move between scenes. Just don't go overboard—nobody needs to see a star wipe every five seconds unless you're making a nostalgic 90s throwback.

Example

In a travel vlog, after showcasing the stunning views of a mountain, you could use a simple fade transition to shift to the next scene at a local café. This gives viewers a moment to digest the scenery before diving into the next adventure, rather than a jarring jump that leaves them wondering if they missed a scene.

Adding Music and Sound Effects

Background music can set the tone of your video and engage viewers. Choose tracks that match the mood—upbeat tunes for fun content and softer melodies for more serious topics. Just be sure to use royalty-free music unless you want your video to be the next viral sensation… for all the wrong reasons.

Example

If you're creating a "day in the life" vlog, using a light, upbeat instrumental track during your morning routine can keep the energy high. As you shift to a more serious segment about a challenge you faced that day, switch to a softer, more reflective piece. This change in music can cue viewers to adjust their emotional responses alongside your content.

Text and Graphics

Adding text overlays or graphics can provide context and highlight key points. Use them sparingly, though! If your video looks like a PowerPoint presentation, viewers might start reminiscing about their last boring meeting instead of focusing on your content.

Example

In a tech review video, when you mention the specs of a device, overlay key terms like "4K Resolution" or "Battery Life: 12 Hours" on the screen. This visual reinforcement helps highlight important information without overwhelming viewers with too much text at once.

Color Correction

Adjusting the color and brightness can make a world of difference. A well-lit video with vibrant colors is far more appealing than one that looks like it was filmed in a cave. Unless, of course, you're aiming for a "mysterious spelunker" vibe—then, by all means, carry on!

Example

If your vlog footage taken indoors looks dull and flat because of poor lighting, use color correction tools to brighten the video and enhance colors. This can make your footage of a lively dinner party pop, making it feel more inviting and engaging.

Tips for Efficient Editing

Organize Your Footage

Keep your files organized in folders by project, date, or content type. This will save you from the chaos of searching for that one clip of your cat wearing a funny hat—trust me, it's worth it!

Example

Create folders for each video project with subfolders labeled "Raw Footage," "B-Roll," "Audio," and "Graphics." If you later decide to create a compilation of your cat's shenanigans, you'll know exactly where to find that elusive footage.

Use Keyboard Shortcuts

Familiarize yourself with keyboard shortcuts for your editing software. They can speed up your workflow and make you feel like a video-editing wizard. Plus, you'll impress your friends when you edit like a pro while they're still trying to figure out how to make a cut.

Example

In Adobe Premiere Pro, using shortcuts like "C" for the Razor tool or "V" to go back to the Selection tool can streamline your editing process. Soon, you'll be slicing through clips like a samurai with a very sharp editing sword—minus the actual sword, of course.

<u>Take Breaks</u>

Editing can be a time-consuming process, and staring at the screen for too long can lead to burnout. Step away, grab a snack, or take a walk. You'll come back with fresh eyes and new ideas—plus, those snacks aren't going to eat themselves!

Example

If you find yourself staring blankly at your timeline for an hour, take a 10-minute break to stretch, hydrate, or indulge in a well-deserved cookie. You might return with a brilliant idea for a fun intro or a clever way to wrap up your video.

Seek Feedback

Once you've completed your edit, don't hesitate to share it with trusted friends or family for feedback. They might catch things you missed—like that awkward moment when you forgot to turn off the camera after filming an intro. (We've all been there!)

Example

Share your finished video with a friend and ask for honest feedback. If they chuckle at the part where you accidentally film your cat instead of the tutorial, consider it a sign to either cut that part or embrace it as a fun blooper reel at the end.

Insights

Mastering the art of editing is essential for creating engaging YouTube content that captivates your audience. By understanding the editing process, utilizing essential techniques, and implementing efficient workflows, you can transform your raw footage into a polished masterpiece. Remember, editing is about storytelling, so embrace your creativity and have fun with it! With practice, a sprinkle of humor, and a few well-timed cuts, you'll soon be on your way to producing videos that not only look great but also resonate with viewers—without leaving them scratching their heads or questioning your sanity. Happy editing!

Tip 7

Optimize Your Video for Success

Congratulations! You've filmed, edited, and crafted your masterpiece. Now, it's time to ensure that all your hard work pays off by optimizing your video for success. Optimization is the process of making your video more discoverable, engaging, and shareable. In this chapter, we'll explore the essential strategies to optimize your videos, helping you attract viewers and keep them coming back for more—without resorting to bribery or delivering pizza to their doorsteps (though that could help).

Understanding Video Optimization

What is Video Optimization?

Video optimization is about making your content more appealing to both viewers and search engines. Think of it as giving your video a digital glow-up, ensuring it shines bright in search results and recommendations. It's like putting a flashy neon sign on your video that says, "Watch me! I'm awesome!"

Why It Matters

With millions of videos uploaded daily, optimization helps your content stand out. Properly optimized videos are more likely to appear in search results, suggested videos, and playlists, increasing your chances of gaining views and subscribers. After all, the goal is to reach an audience that's as excited about your content as a kid in a candy store.

Key Strategies for Video Optimization

Craft an Engaging Title

We've covered this before, but it bears repeating. Your title should be catchy, descriptive, and include relevant keywords. A good title not only informs viewers about the content but also grabs their attention.

Example

Instead of "Cooking Video #3," try "10-Minute Spaghetti Carbonara: Quick & Delicious!" This title tells viewers exactly what to expect and highlights the video's appeal.

Write a Detailed Description

Your video description should provide context and include relevant keywords. Use the first few lines to summarize the video since those will often show up in search results. Then, expand on the content, include links to your social media, and invite viewers to subscribe.

Example
"In this video, I'll show you how to make a quick and delicious spaghetti carbonara in just 10 minutes! Perfect for busy weeknights. Don't forget to check out my other pasta recipes and subscribe for more easy meals!" 3.

Use Tags Wisely

Tags help YouTube understand the content of your video. Use a mix of broad and specific tags that relate to your video. Think of tags as the keywords that help your video get discovered. Just don't go overboard—spamming tags won't win you any friends, and it certainly won't help your video.

Example
For the spaghetti video, you might use tags like "spaghetti carbonara," "quick recipes," "easy pasta dishes," and "cooking tips." This helps YouTube categorize your video and suggest it to interested viewers.

Create Eye-Catching Thumbnails

We discussed thumbnails earlier, but they are worth mentioning again! A visually appealing thumbnail can significantly increase your click-through rate. Make sure it's relevant to your content and stands out from the crowd.

Example

Use a high-quality image of the finished dish, add some bold text like "10-Minute Recipe!" and use bright colors to make it pop. If it looks appetizing, viewers will be more likely to click!

Add Closed Captions

Including closed captions can enhance accessibility and improve viewer engagement. Not only does it help those who are hard of hearing, but it also allows viewers to watch your video in noisy environments (like a crowded coffee shop) without missing a beat.

Example

You can either create captions manually or use YouTube's auto-captioning feature, then edit for accuracy. This small effort can make a big difference in reaching a broader audience.

Promote Your Video

Share on Social Media

Once your video is live, promote it across your social media platforms. Share snippets, behind-the-scenes clips, or engaging graphics to grab attention. The more eyes on your video, the better!

Example

Create a short teaser clip for Instagram Stories or a fun post for Facebook that highlights a funny moment from your video. Encourage your followers to check it out, and remind them to subscribe for more content.

Engage with Your Audience

Encourage viewers to like, comment, and share your video. Respond to comments to build a community and foster engagement. A little interaction can go a long way in making viewers feel valued.

Example

At the end of your video, ask viewers to share their favorite quick recipes in the comments or let them know that you'll be responding to comments in the first hour after posting. This can create a buzz and encourage more engagement.

Collaborate with Other Creators

Partnering with other YouTubers in your niche can introduce your content to new audiences. Consider collaborating on videos, shout-outs, or even guest appearances.

Example

If you're a cooking channel, collaborate with a nutritionist to create a video on healthy meal prep. This not only adds value to your audience but also exposes you to the nutritionist's viewers.

Analyze and Adjust

Monitor Your Analytics

Keep an eye on your YouTube analytics to see how your videos are performing. Look for metrics like watch time, audience retention, and click-through rates to understand what works and what doesn't.

Example

If you notice that viewers are dropping off at a certain point in your video, consider adjusting your content or pacing in future videos to keep them engaged.

Experiment with Different Formats

Don't be afraid to try new things! Experiment with different video formats, lengths, or styles to see what resonates most with your audience. Sometimes, a little variety can spice up your channel like a dash of hot sauce on a bland dish.

Example

If your cooking tutorials are performing well, try adding a "Cooking Challenge" video where you attempt to make a meal with random ingredients. This adds an element of fun and spontaneity that viewers may love!

Insights

Optimizing your videos is essential for ensuring your hard work reaches a wider audience. By crafting engaging titles, writing detailed descriptions, using relevant tags, creating eye-catching thumbnails, and promoting your content effectively, you'll increase your chances of success on YouTube. Remember, video optimization is an ongoing process—don't hesitate to analyze your performance and adjust your strategy as needed. With a sprinkle of humor and a dash of creativity, you'll be well on your way to building a thriving YouTube channel that keeps viewers coming back for seconds!

Tip 8

Build Your Community

Welcome to the chapter dedicated to building your community on YouTube! It's time to transform your channel from a solitary endeavor into a vibrant hub of engagement and interaction. A strong community not only enhances your channel's growth but also makes the whole experience more enjoyable—for you and your viewers. After all, who doesn't want to hang out with a bunch of people who share their love for cat videos and cooking hacks? Let's dive into how to cultivate that community spirit, one subscriber at a time!

Understanding the Importance of Community

The Power of Connection

In the vast ocean of YouTube, having a loyal community can keep you afloat. Viewers who feel a connection with you are more likely to engage with your content, share it, and come back for more. It's like having a fan club, minus the awkward membership cards and secret handshakes.

Feedback and Growth

A community provides valuable feedback that can help you improve your content. Your viewers might have ideas or suggestions that never crossed your mind—like that time you thought a video on "How to Cook Pasta" was groundbreaking, but they really wanted to see "How to Cook Pasta While Juggling." (Challenge accepted!)

Strategies for Building Your Community

Engage with Your Audience

Responding to comments is one of the simplest yet most effective ways to build a community. When viewers see that you're interacting with them and valuing their input, they're more likely to stick around.

Example

If someone comments, "This recipe was amazing! My family loved it!" respond with something like, "I'm so glad they enjoyed it! What's their favorite dish? I might just steal it for my next video!" This not only shows appreciation but also invites further conversation.

Create a Call to Action

At the end of your videos, encourage viewers to subscribe, like, and comment. Make it fun! Instead of the usual "Don't forget to subscribe," you could say, "If you enjoyed this video, hit that subscribe button like you're slapping a mosquito on a hot summer day!"

Host Live Streams

Live streaming is a fantastic way to connect with your audience in real-time. It's like throwing a virtual party where everyone's invited and nobody has to worry about awkward small talk by the snack table.

Example
Host a Q&A session where viewers can ask you anything about your cooking techniques, your favorite kitchen disasters, or even your secret for not burning toast. Just be prepared for that one person who might ask about your favorite dinosaur—because, you know, the internet.

Utilize Social Media

Promote your channel and engage with your audience on social media platforms like Instagram, Twitter, or Facebook. Share behind-the-scenes content, sneak peeks of upcoming videos, or even polls to get your audience involved.

Example

Post a poll on Instagram asking, "What should I cook next: Spicy Tacos or Delightful Desserts?" The winning dish can become your next video! Plus, your audience will feel like they played a part in the decision-making process—like they're the judges on a cooking show, but without the weird tension.

Create a Community Tab

Once you reach a certain number of subscribers, you can utilize the Community tab to share updates, polls, and engage with your audience. It's like having a digital bulletin board, but way cooler!

Example

Post fun memes, ask for feedback on video ideas, or share personal anecdotes. You could even create a weekly "Fan Feature" where you highlight a viewer's comment or content, making them feel like a superstar.

Foster a Positive Environment

Moderate Comments

Keep an eye on your comment section to ensure it stays a positive space. If trolls come out to play, don't hesitate to wield the mighty banhammer. Remember, you want your community to feel welcoming, not like a battlefield.

Example
If someone leaves a negative comment, respond with grace or, if necessary, a polite reminder of your channel's positivity policy. You might say, "Thanks for your input! How about we keep this channel a happy place for cookie lovers?"

Encourage Collaboration

Collaborating with other creators can introduce your channel to new audiences and build a sense of community among creators. It's like forming a supergroup, but instead of rockstars, you've got chefs, gamers, and DIY enthusiasts.

Example
Team up with another YouTuber for a cooking challenge where you both try to make the same dish in your unique styles. Your audiences will love seeing how different creators tackle the same challenge, and it can lead to some hilarious moments!

Celebrate Milestones Together

Share your achievements with your community! Whether you hit a subscriber milestone or receive a nice comment, celebrate it with your viewers. It's like throwing a virtual party, and everyone loves a good reason to celebrate—especially if cake is involved.

Example

Create a special video thanking your subscribers for their support and sharing some funny moments from your journey. You might even bake a cake (or order one, no judgment here) to commemorate the occasion and show that you appreciate their contributions.

Insights

Building a community around your YouTube channel is essential for long-term success and fulfillment. By engaging with your audience, utilizing social media, hosting live streams, and fostering a positive environment, you can create a space where viewers feel connected and valued. Remember, a strong community doesn't just happen overnight—it takes time, effort, and a sprinkle of humor to cultivate. With the right approach, you'll transform your channel into a thriving hub of creativity and camaraderie, making your YouTube journey all the more rewarding. Now, go forth and let your community flourish like a well-watered houseplant—preferably one that doesn't die on you after a week!

Tip 9

Analyze Your Performance

Now that you've built a thriving community and created some amazing videos, it's time to take a step back and analyze how everything is performing. Understanding your analytics can be the secret sauce to improving your content and growing your channel. Think of it as your personal treasure map, guiding you toward that pot of gold—otherwise known as increased views, subscribers, and engagement.

Let's dive into the world of YouTube analytics and uncover insights that can elevate your channel!

Understanding YouTube Analytics

What Are YouTube Analytics?

YouTube Analytics is a powerful tool that provides you with detailed insights into your channel's performance. It shows you everything from how many views your videos are getting to where your audience is located. It's like having a crystal ball that reveals the preferences and behaviors of your viewers—minus the mysterious fog and fortune-teller vibes.

Why It Matters

Analyzing your performance helps you understand what's working, what's not, and where you can improve. By paying attention to your analytics, you can make informed decisions about your content strategy, ensuring that you're creating videos that resonate with your audience. It's basically the cheat sheet for leveling up your YouTube game!

Key Metrics to Monitor

Views

The most straightforward metric, views show you how many times your video has been watched. It's like the score of a game—everyone wants to see those numbers climb!

Example

If your latest cooking tutorial gets 10,000 views, but your previous video only got 1,000, take note! What made this video more appealing? Was it the title, thumbnail, or perhaps the secret ingredient you revealed?

Watch Time

This metric tells you how long viewers are watching your video on average. It's crucial because YouTube favors videos with higher watch time, which can lead to better rankings and more visibility.

Example

If your watch time is significantly lower than expected, it might be time to reevaluate your content. Did you start with a long intro? Are there sections where viewers lose interest? Consider tightening up those parts for future videos.

Audience Retention

This shows you the percentage of your video that viewers watch on average. A high retention rate indicates that your content is engaging and keeps viewers hooked. If your audience retention drops sharply at a specific point, it's like a flashing neon sign saying, "Fix this part!"

Example

If you notice that viewers drop off right before the big reveal in your cooking video, consider moving that part earlier or making the lead-up more exciting. Maybe sprinkle in some suspenseful music or a cheeky tease!

Click-Through Rate (CTR)

Your CTR measures how many people clicked on your video after seeing the thumbnail and title. A low CTR might indicate that your thumbnail or title isn't enticing enough, while a high CTR suggests you've nailed the art of getting people to click.

Example

If your "Delicious Chocolate Cake" video has a low CTR, it could be time to rethink your thumbnail. Perhaps a mouth-watering close-up of the cake with the words "Irresistibly Decadent!" could lure in more cake lovers.

Demographics

Understanding who your audience is can help tailor your content to their preferences. You can see things like age, gender, and geographic location, which can inform your approach.

Example

If you discover that a significant portion of your audience is between 18-24 and located in a particular country, you might consider creating content that resonates with their culture or preferences—like trendy recipes or popular local dishes.

Using Analytics to Improve Content.

Identify Trends

Monitor which types of videos perform best over time. Are your recipe videos getting more views compared to vlogs? Use this information to adjust your content strategy accordingly.

Example

If you notice that your "Quick Breakfast Recipes" video consistently outperforms others, consider creating a series around quick meals for busy mornings—because who doesn't need a little help when they're running late?

Experiment and Iterate

Don't be afraid to experiment with different formats, styles, or topics based on your findings. YouTube is a platform that rewards creativity, so mix things up and see how your audience responds.

Example

If you usually do straightforward recipe tutorials but notice a trend in trending food challenges, try incorporating a fun challenge into your cooking videos. Who knows? Your "Cooking with Mystery Ingredients" video could go viral!

Set Goals

Use your analytics to set realistic goals for your channel. Whether it's increasing your watch time, improving your CTR, or gaining more subscribers, having clear objectives can help keep you focused and motivated.

Example

If your goal is to increase your average watch time by 30% over the next three months, analyze your current content and brainstorm ways to keep viewers engaged longer—like adding exciting graphics, storytelling elements, or even a blooper reel at the end.

Insights

Analyzing your performance on YouTube is crucial for understanding what resonates with your audience and improving your content. By monitoring key metrics like views, watch time, audience retention, CTR, and demographics, you can make informed decisions that drive growth. Remember, analytics is not just a bunch of numbers; it's a treasure trove of insights waiting to be uncovered. So put on your detective hat, dive into those metrics, and let them guide you toward creating even more engaging content. With a little wit, creativity, and a willingness to adapt, you'll be well on your way to YouTube success—one click at a time!

Tip 10

Monetization Strategies

Ah, the sweet sound of coins clinking! Welcome to the chapter where we discuss monetization strategies for your YouTube channel. Turning your passion for creating content into a source of income can feel like hitting the jackpot—especially when you realize you can fund your coffee habit or even your dream vacation with those YouTube earnings. In this chapter, we'll explore various ways to monetize your channel and help you turn those views into dollars—without resorting to selling your old Pokémon cards (unless that's your thing, then go for it!).

Understanding YouTube Monetization

What is Monetization?

Monetization refers to the process of earning money from your content. YouTube offers several ways to monetize your channel, from ad revenue to sponsored content, merchandise sales, and more. It's like having a buffet of income options—just make sure you don't overindulge and get a stomachache!

Eligibility for Monetization

To start earning money through YouTube ads, you need to join the YouTube Partner Program (YPP). Currently, you must have at least 1,000 subscribers and 4,000 watch hours in the past 12 months. Think of these as the golden keys that unlock the treasure chest of monetization.

Ad Revenue

This is the most common way to monetize your channel. Once you're part of the YouTube Partner Program, you can enable ads on your videos. You earn money based on clicks and views of those ads—kind of like getting paid to let people interrupt your content!

Example
If you post a cooking video and run ads, every time someone watches the ad before your tutorial, you earn a small amount of revenue. While it may not fund a yacht right away, those pennies can add up over time!

Channel Memberships

If you have a loyal following, consider offering channel memberships. This allows viewers to support you monthly in exchange for exclusive perks like custom badges, emojis, or members-only content. It's like creating a VIP club where your biggest fans can hang out—just without the velvet ropes.

Example

If you run a baking channel, you might offer members exclusive access to live baking sessions, early video releases, or special recipes that aren't available to the public. Your super fans will love it!

Super Chat and Super Stickers

If you live stream, these features allow your viewers to pay to have their messages highlighted in the chat. It's like a digital tip jar, where fans can show their appreciation while you're live—and it's always nice to see a little love when you're in the middle of a chaotic cooking demonstration!

Example

During a live cooking stream, a viewer might send you a Super Chat saying, "I love your recipes! Can you make a vegan lasagna next?" Not only does it give you a boost, but it also provides you with content ideas!

Sponsored Content

Partnering with brands can be a lucrative way to monetize your channel. You can create videos that promote products or services in exchange for payment. Just make sure to disclose these partnerships to your audience—transparency is key!

Example

If you collaborate with a kitchen appliance company, you might create a video showcasing their blender while demonstrating a smoothie recipe. Just remember to keep it authentic; viewers appreciate honest reviews more than a forced sales pitch.

Merchandise Sales

If you have a strong brand or catchphrase, consider selling merchandise! T-shirts, mugs, or cooking tools with your logo or fun sayings can add an extra revenue stream while allowing your fans to show their support (and maybe start a new trend).

Example

If your channel is all about quick recipes, you could sell cutting boards with the slogan "Chop It Like It's Hot!" Your fans will love repping your brand in their kitchens.

Affiliate Marketing

This involves promoting products or services and earning a commission for every sale made through your unique affiliate link. It's a win-win: you share products you love, and you get paid for it!

Example
If you recommend a specific brand of cooking utensils in your video, include an affiliate link in the description. If viewers purchase through that link, you earn a percentage of the sale—no extra effort required!

Tips for Successful Monetization

Stay Authentic

Whether you're running ads or promoting products, authenticity is crucial. Your audience trusts you, so make sure to promote products you genuinely believe in. If they feel like you're just in it for the money, they might start to tune out—like a friend who only calls when they need help moving.

Diversify Your Income Streams

Don't rely solely on one method of monetization. The more diverse your income streams, the more secure your financial situation will be. It's like not putting all your eggs in one basket—especially if you're known for dropping things!

Engage with Your Audience

Building a strong community can lead to higher engagement and support for your monetization efforts. The more connected your audience feels, the more likely they are to support you through memberships, merch, or sharing your videos.

Keep Learning

Stay informed about changes in YouTube's policies and best practices for monetization. The platform is constantly evolving, and being adaptable can help you stay ahead of the game.

Insights

Monetizing your YouTube channel is an exciting journey that allows you to turn your passion for creating content into a source of income. By exploring various monetization methods such as ad revenue, channel memberships, sponsored content, merchandise sales, and affiliate marketing, you can find the right mix that works for you. Remember to stay authentic, diversify your income streams, and engage with your audience along the way. With a little creativity, determination, and a sense of humor, you'll be well on your way to transforming your YouTube hobby into a thriving business—without needing to resort to bake sales or lemonade stands!

Tip 11

Stay Consistent and Evolve

Welcome to the chapter that emphasizes the importance of consistency and evolution in your YouTube journey! In the ever-changing landscape of online content creation, staying consistent while adapting to new trends can be the key to long-term success. Think of it as riding a wave: if you want to stay on your board and not wipe out, you need to find that perfect balance between sticking to your style and being open to new possibilities. Let's explore how to maintain consistency and embrace evolution without losing your creative spark!

The Importance of Consistency

Building Trust

Consistency is crucial for building trust with your audience. When viewers know they can rely on you to deliver quality content on a regular schedule, it fosters loyalty and keeps them coming back for more. It's like having a favorite café that always serves your go-to coffee—if they suddenly decide to close for a month, you might just have to find a new spot (which is a tragedy we want to avoid).

Algorithm Favor

The YouTube algorithm loves consistency. Regular uploads improve your chances of being recommended to new viewers, enhancing your visibility and growth. Think of it as feeding the algorithm; the more you feed it (with great content), the happier it becomes!

Example

If you decide to upload once a week, stick to that schedule. Your audience will come to expect new content every Tuesday, and the algorithm will recognize your commitment, potentially boosting your videos in search results.

Creating a Brand

Consistent content helps to establish your brand identity. Whether it's your video style, catchphrases, or visual elements, having a recognizable "look" can set you apart from the competition. It's like your personal signature—distinct, memorable, and totally you!

Strategies for Staying Consistent

Set a Content Schedule

Create a realistic upload schedule that you can stick to. Whether it's weekly, bi-weekly, or monthly, consistency is key. Just remember: quality over quantity! It's better to produce one amazing video a month than five rushed ones that leave viewers scratching their heads.

Example
If you decide on a weekly schedule, choose a specific day and time (e.g., every Wednesday at 5 PM). This way, your audience knows when to tune in, just like waiting for their favorite TV show to air.

Batch Production

Consider filming multiple videos in one session to stay ahead of your schedule. This way, you won't find yourself scrambling for content at the last minute. Plus, you can wear the same outfit in all your videos and pretend you filmed them on different days—instant time travel!

Example
If you're planning a series on healthy snacks, spend a day filming all the recipes at once. You can then edit them gradually, ensuring you always have content ready to go.

Plan Your Content

Create a content calendar to map out topics and video ideas for the upcoming weeks or months. This helps you stay organized and ensures you always have a plan in place.

Example

If you know that the holiday season is approaching, plan festive recipes or gift ideas ahead of time. This way, you'll be prepared and can capitalize on seasonal trends. #### Embracing Evolution

Stay Informed

The digital landscape is always changing, with new trends, platforms, and audience preferences emerging regularly. Stay up to date on industry news, popular content trends, and viewer feedback to adapt your strategy.

Example

If short-form videos like YouTube Shorts become increasingly popular, consider incorporating them into your content strategy. Experimenting with new formats can attract a wider audience and keep your content fresh.

Seek Feedback

Encourage feedback from your audience to understand what they love and what they'd like to see more of. This can guide your evolution while ensuring you remain in tune with your viewers' preferences.

Example

After a few cooking videos, ask your audience in the comments or on social media what type of recipes they want next. If they're clamoring for more vegan options, consider branching out—without losing your signature style!

Experiment with Content

Don't be afraid to try new styles, formats, or topics. Evolution is about growth, and stepping outside your comfort zone can lead to exciting opportunities. Just remember, every great chef has to try a few odd flavor combinations before finding the perfect recipe.

Example

If you typically do traditional recipe videos, challenge yourself to create a "mukbang" or a "cook and chat" video where you prepare food while sharing personal stories. This can engage your audience in a new way and showcase your personality!

Reflect and Adapt

Regularly assess your content and performance. If you notice certain types of videos resonate more with your audience, consider creating more of that content. Adaptability is key in a fast-paced environment like YouTube.

Example

If your "30-Minute Meals" video performs exceptionally well, you might want to explore a series focusing on time-saving kitchen tips. Your audience will appreciate your responsiveness, and it may lead to increased engagement.

Insight

Staying consistent while embracing evolution is essential for long-term success on YouTube. By building trust with your audience, optimizing your content strategy, and remaining open to change, you can create a channel that thrives in an ever-evolving digital landscape. Remember, it's not just about sticking to a routine; it's about finding that sweet spot where consistency meets creativity. With a dash of determination and a sprinkle of innovation, you'll ride the waves of YouTube like a pro—without ever wiping out! Now, go forth and continue creating, learning, and evolving!

Tip 12

Navigating Challenges and Setbacks

Welcome to the chapter that addresses the inevitable bumps in the road—challenges and setbacks that can come your way on your YouTube journey. Let's face it: even the most successful creators have faced moments of doubt, technical glitches, and creative blocks. The key is not to let these challenges derail your passion or enthusiasm. Instead, consider them opportunities for growth, resilience, and maybe a bit of hilarity along the way. After all, who doesn't love a good comeback story?

Understanding Common Challenges

Creative Burnout

Producing content week after week can lead to burnout, where you feel drained and uninspired. It's like running a marathon without a water station—eventually, you need a break to recharge!

Negative Feedback

Not everyone will love your content, and negative comments can sting. While constructive criticism can be helpful, harsh or rude remarks can feel like a punch to the gut. Remember, the internet can be a wild place with keyboard warriors lurking around every corner.

Technical Issues

From video editing software crashing to audio glitches, technical challenges can be frustrating. It's like finally getting ready for a big presentation only for the projector to malfunction—cue the panic!

Plateauing Growth

At times, you might notice your subscriber count or views stagnating. It can feel disheartening, like running in place while everyone else zooms ahead. But remember, growth is not always linear!

Strategies for Overcoming Challenges

Recognize and Address Burnout

If you're feeling overwhelmed, take a step back. It's okay to take a break or reduce your posting frequency. Use this time to recharge, find inspiration, and explore new interests.

Example
If you typically post weekly, consider taking a month off to explore new recipes, travel, or just binge-watch your favorite shows. You might return with fresh ideas and a renewed passion for creating content.

Embrace Constructive Criticism

Learn to differentiate between constructive feedback and negativity. Use constructive comments to improve your content, while ignoring the trolls. Remember, for every negative comment, there are likely many viewers who appreciate your work.

Example
If a viewer suggests that your lighting could be better, take it as an opportunity to invest in some affordable softbox lights. On the other hand, if someone comments "You should quit!" just remember that everyone has an opinion—even the ones who can't cook a frozen pizza.

Troubleshoot Technical Issues

Familiarize yourself with basic troubleshooting for common technical problems. Have backup plans in place, like saving your work frequently and keeping extra equipment on hand.

Example

If your editing software crashes, ensure you save your project regularly. If you're using a microphone, invest in a backup just in case it decides to stop working mid-video. You never know when tech will throw a tantrum!

Celebrate Small Wins

Acknowledge your accomplishments, no matter how small. Celebrating milestones can boost your motivation and remind you that progress is being made, even when it feels slow.

Example

If you hit a small milestone like 500 subscribers or receive a particularly positive comment, celebrate it! Maybe treat yourself to a nice meal or share the news with your community. It's all about those little victories!

Seek Support

Don't hesitate to reach out to fellow creators or friends for support. Joining online communities or forums can provide encouragement and valuable insights. Remember, you're not alone on this journey.

Example
Connect with other YouTubers in your niche through social media or forums. Share experiences and tips, or even collaborate on a project. It's like having a support group—minus the awkward sharing circle.

Reassess Your Strategy

If you notice growth plateauing, take a moment to reassess your content strategy. Explore new topics, formats, or styles that might reinvigorate your channel.

Example
If you've primarily focused on recipe videos, consider branching into cooking challenges or lifestyle vlogs. Experimenting with different content can attract new viewers and keep your existing audience engaged.

Maintaining a Positive Mindset

Prioritize your mental and physical well-being. Engage in activities that make you feel good, whether it's exercising, spending time with loved ones, or indulging in hobbies outside of YouTube.

Stay Focused on Your Passion

Remember why you started creating content in the first place. Reconnect with your passion for cooking, storytelling, or whatever brought you to YouTube. This can provide motivation during tough times.

Example
Rewatch your favorite videos that inspired you to start your channel. Let that excitement reignite your creative flames as you dive back into content creation.

Laugh at the Blunders

Embrace the humorous moments and setbacks. Sometimes, the best stories come from things going hilariously wrong. Sharing your bloopers or mishaps can connect you with your audience on a deeper level.

Example

If you accidentally added salt instead of sugar to a recipe, share that moment in your next video. Your audience will appreciate your authenticity and humor, and it may even become a running joke in your community.

Insights

Navigating challenges and setbacks is an inevitable part of the YouTube journey, but how you respond can make all the difference. By recognizing and addressing burnout, embracing constructive criticism, troubleshooting technical issues, celebrating small wins, seeking support, and maintaining a positive mindset, you can overcome obstacles and continue growing. Remember, every setback can lead to a comeback, and every challenge is an opportunity for growth. With resilience, a sense of humor, and a dash of creativity, you'll not only navigate the tough times but emerge stronger and more inspired than ever. Now, go forth and conquer those challenges like the YouTube warrior you are!

Tip 13

Leveraging Trends and Collaboration

Welcome to the chapter where we explore the exciting world of trends and collaboration! In the fast-paced realm of YouTube, staying relevant often means tapping into current trends and teaming up with fellow creators. Think of it as riding the wave of popularity while holding hands with a friend—way more fun and a lot less likely to result in a wipeout. Let's dive into how you can identify trends, collaborate effectively, and make the most of these strategies to enhance your channel!

Understanding Trends

What Are Trends?

Trends are popular topics, challenges, or themes that capture the attention of viewers at any given time. These can range from viral challenges to seasonal themes and hot topics in the culinary world. Jumping on trends can increase your visibility and attract new subscribers.

Why Trends Matter

Engaging with trends can help keep your content fresh and relevant. It allows you to tap into the conversations that people are already having, making it easier to connect with a wider audience. Plus, who doesn't love being part of the latest viral sensation?

How to Identify Trends

YouTube Trends Dashboard

Utilize YouTube's trending page to see what videos are gaining traction. This can provide insights into popular topics and formats that you might consider incorporating into your content.

Example
 If you notice a surge in cooking videos featuring air fryers, it might be time to create your own air fryer recipe tutorial.

Social Media Listening

Platforms like Twitter, Instagram, and TikTok can be great for spotting trends. Follow hashtags related to your niche and pay attention to what's being discussed.

Example

If you see a lot of buzz around a specific ingredient or cooking technique, consider creating content that showcases your own take on it.

Community Engagement

Interact with your audience and ask them about their interests or what they'd like to see next. This not only informs you about trending topics but also makes your viewers feel valued and involved.

Example

Post a poll on your community tab asking, "What kind of recipes do you want to see next? A) Vegan, B) Desserts, C) Quick Meals." The results can guide your upcoming content.

Collaborating with Other Creators

Why Collaborate?

Collaborations can introduce your channel to new audiences, provide fresh perspectives, and enhance your content. It's like throwing a potluck dinner—everyone brings something to the table, and the feast is way more enjoyable!

Finding the Right Collaborators

Look for creators who share a similar audience or niche. This ensures that the collaboration feels natural and resonates with both of your followers.

Example

If you're a cooking channel, consider collaborating with a nutritionist to create healthy recipes. This adds value to both your audiences and can attract new viewers.

Reach Out Professionally

When approaching potential collaborators, be clear about your ideas and what you hope to achieve together. A well-crafted message can make all the difference.

Example

Send a friendly email or message saying something like, "Hey [Creator's Name]! I love your content on [specific aspect]. I think it would be great to collaborate on a video about [specific idea]! Let me know if you're interested!"

Plan the Collaboration

Once you've agreed to collaborate, plan the details. Discuss the format, content, and promotion strategies to ensure a smooth experience.

Example

If you're shooting a joint cooking video, decide who will handle filming, editing, and promotion. This way, everyone knows their roles, and the process feels more organized.

Promote Each Other

After the collaboration, promote it across both channels. Share clips, behind-the-scenes content, and links to the full video. This maximizes exposure and encourages viewers to check out both creators.

Example

Create teaser clips for your social media platforms, tagging your collaborator and encouraging your audience to watch the full video on their channel.

Making the Most of Trends and Collaborations

Stay Authentic

While it's great to jump on trends, make sure to infuse your unique personality and style into your content. Authenticity will resonate more with your audience than simply following a trend for the sake of it.

Example

If you're participating in a viral cooking challenge, add your own twist—maybe a signature ingredient or a humorous commentary—to make it distinctly yours.

Monitor Engagement

After you've jumped on a trend or completed a collaboration, keep an eye on how your audience responds. This feedback can inform your future content decisions.

Example

If your air fryer recipe video receives a lot of engagement, consider making it a series. Your audience will appreciate the consistency and know what to expect.

Be Open to New Ideas

Trends and collaborations can spark new ideas you hadn't considered before. Stay flexible and willing to explore new content directions that may arise from these experiences.

Example

If a collaboration leads to discussions about healthy eating, you might decide to create a mini-series focused on nutritious recipes, expanding your content beyond your usual offerings.

Insights

Leveraging trends and collaboration is a powerful way to enhance your YouTube channel and engage with a broader audience. By identifying current trends, collaborating with other creators, and staying true to your unique style, you can create dynamic content that resonates with viewers. Remember, the key is to ride the wave of popularity while maintaining your individuality—because at the end of the day, it's your unique voice that will keep viewers coming back for more. So grab your surfboard, embrace the trends, and enjoy the collaborative journey ahead!

Tip 14

Building Your Brand Beyond

YouTube Welcome to the chapter that takes you beyond the realm of YouTube and into the exciting world of personal branding! Building a brand that extends beyond your YouTube channel can create new opportunities, diversify your income, and solidify your presence in the digital space. Think of it as planting seeds in different gardens—each one has the potential to flourish and yield delicious fruits! Let's explore how to cultivate your brand across various platforms and avenues.

Understanding Personal Branding

What is Personal Branding?

Personal branding is the practice of marketing yourself and your career as a brand. It encompasses your values, skills, and unique qualities that differentiate you from others in your niche. Essentially, it's how you present yourself to the world—like a beautifully packaged product waiting to be unwrapped!

Why It Matters

A strong personal brand helps establish credibility, attract new opportunities, and create a loyal following. It allows you to connect with your audience on a deeper level and can lead to collaborations, sponsorships, and even book deals. Plus, it gives you the power to shape how people perceive you in the digital landscape.

Expanding Your Brand

Create a Website

Having a personal website can serve as a central hub for your brand. It allows you to showcase your content, share your story, and provide information about what you offer beyond YouTube.

Example

Use your website to host a blog, share recipes, and provide resources like e-books or cooking classes. This can enhance your credibility and give your audience more ways to engage with your content.

Leverage Social Media

Use platforms like Instagram, Twitter, Facebook, and TikTok to extend your reach and engage with your audience in different ways. Each platform offers unique opportunities to connect and share your content.

Example
Share behind-the-scenes photos of your cooking process on Instagram, engage in real-time conversations on Twitter, or create quick recipe videos on TikTok. Tailor your content to fit the platform while maintaining your brand identity.

Email Marketing

Building an email list is a fantastic way to keep your audience updated on new content, special offers, and upcoming projects. It's like having a direct line to your fans, ensuring they never miss out on what you're up to!

Example
Offer a free downloadable recipe e-book in exchange for email sign-ups. Use your email newsletter to share exclusive content, cooking tips, or news about upcoming videos.

Diversify Your Content

Consider expanding your content offerings beyond YouTube videos. This could include writing a cookbook, launching a podcast, or creating online courses. The more diverse your content, the more ways you can connect with your audience.

Example

If you're passionate about healthy cooking, consider writing a cookbook filled with your favorite recipes or launching a podcast where you interview other chefs and food enthusiasts.

Merchandising

If you have a strong brand identity, consider creating merchandise that reflects your style and resonates with your audience. This can include anything from branded kitchen tools to clothing featuring catchy phrases or your logo.

Example

If your channel focuses on fun, quick recipes, consider selling aprons or kitchen gadgets that align with your brand. Your fans will appreciate the opportunity to show their support in a tangible way!

Networking and Collaborations

Attend Events and Workshops

Participate in food festivals, cooking workshops, or industry conferences to network with other creators and industry professionals. Building relationships can lead to collaborative opportunities and expand your reach.

Example
Attend a local food festival to meet other chefs and influencers. Share your experiences on social media, and don't hesitate to collaborate with those you meet!

Join Online Communities

Engage with fellow creators and audiences in online forums, Facebook groups, or Reddit communities related to your niche. Sharing knowledge and experiences can enhance your brand and foster valuable connections.

Example
Join a cooking or food blogging group where you can exchange ideas, seek feedback, and support one another in your creative endeavors.

Maintaining Your Brand Identity

Stay True to Yourself

As you expand your brand, ensure that everything you do aligns with your values and personality. Authenticity is key to building trust with your audience, and they'll appreciate your genuine approach.

Example

If you're known for your humorous cooking style, keep that tone consistent across all platforms. Your audience will recognize and appreciate the familiar vibe.

Engage with Your Audience

Continue to interact with your followers and value their feedback. Building a community around your brand can enhance loyalty and keep your audience engaged.

Example

Respond to comments on your social media posts, ask for input on new content ideas, and create opportunities for your audience to participate in your journey.

Evolve as You Grow

As your brand expands, be open to evolving your style and content. Keep an eye on trends and be willing to adapt while still staying true to your core identity.

Example

If you find that your audience is increasingly interested in plant-based recipes, consider incorporating more of those into your content while still sharing your signature dishes.

Insights

Building your brand beyond YouTube is an exciting venture that can open new doors and create lasting connections with your audience. By creating a website, leveraging social media, diversifying your content, networking, and maintaining your authenticity, you can cultivate a strong personal brand that resonates with viewers. Remember, your brand is an extension of you—so let it shine brightly across all platforms! With a sprinkle of creativity and a dash of determination, you'll be well on your way to establishing a brand that goes beyond your YouTube channel. Now, go forth and plant those seeds in every garden, and watch your brand flourish!

Tip 15

Analyzing Your Growth and Metrics

Welcome to the chapter where we delve into the world of analytics and metrics—your roadmap to understanding your growth and improving your content on YouTube! While creating content is undoubtedly exciting, analyzing performance data can provide you with valuable insights that will help you refine your strategy and ultimately boost your success. Let's explore the essential metrics to monitor, how to analyze your growth, and the steps you can take to make informed decisions based on your findings.

Understanding YouTube Analytics

What is YouTube Analytics?

YouTube Analytics is a powerful tool provided by the platform that offers insights into your channel's performance, viewer engagement, and audience demographics. It's like having a treasure map that reveals where your gold is hidden—if you know how to read it!

Why It Matters

By tracking your analytics, you can identify what works, what doesn't, and how to optimize your content for better results. This data-driven approach allows you to make informed decisions that can enhance your channel's growth.

Key Metrics to Monitor

Views

The total number of times your videos have been viewed. While views are an important metric, they should be considered alongside other factors, such as engagement and watch time.

Example
If a video garners a high number of views but low engagement, it may indicate that the content didn't resonate as well as expected.

Watch Time

The total number of minutes viewers have spent watching your videos. High watch time indicates that your content is engaging and keeps viewers interested. **Example**: If your watch time is significantly lower than the number of views, it may suggest that viewers are clicking away before the video ends, prompting you to reevaluate your pacing or content structure.

Audience Retention

This metric shows the percentage of your video that viewers watch on average. It's crucial for understanding how well your content holds attention.

Example
If you notice a sharp drop in audience retention at a specific point in your video, consider revisiting that section to make it more engaging or concise.

Click-Through Rate (CTR)

The percentage of people who clicked on your video after seeing the thumbnail and title. A high CTR indicates that your title and thumbnail are effective at catching viewers' attention.

Example
If your video has a low CTR, it may be time to experiment with different thumbnails or titles to better attract viewers.

Engagement Metrics

This includes likes, comments, shares, and subscriptions gained from each video. High engagement indicates that viewers are not only watching but also interacting with your content.

Example

If a particular video receives a lot of comments and shares, analyze what made it resonate with your audience. Did you cover a trending topic, or was the content particularly relatable?

Demographics

Understanding who your audience is can inform your content strategy. You can see data on age, gender, and location, which can guide you in tailoring your content to better serve your viewers.

Example

If you discover that a significant portion of your audience is in a specific age group, you might consider creating content that appeals specifically to their interests.

Analyzing Your Growth

Set Goals

Establish clear and measurable goals for your channel. This could include targets for subscribers, views, watch time, or engagement metrics.

Example
You might set a goal to achieve 1,000 new subscribers within three months. Having specific goals helps you stay focused and motivated.

Monitor Trends Over Time

Regularly check your analytics to identify trends in your performance. Look for patterns in which videos perform best and why.

Example
If cooking tutorials consistently perform better than vlogs, you may want to focus more on that format in your future content.

Evaluate Content Performance

Assess the performance of individual videos to understand what resonates with your audience. Look for common elements in high-performing videos, such as topics, presentation style, or video length.

Example
If your "Quick and Easy Dinner Recipes" video receives high engagement, consider creating a series around quick meals or time-saving cooking tips.

Adjust Your Strategy

Use the insights gained from your analytics to refine your content strategy. If certain types of videos are underperforming, consider adjusting your approach or exploring new topics.

Example
If your audience retention drops significantly in longer videos, try creating shorter, more concise content to keep viewers engaged.

Making Informed Decisions

Experiment and Iterate

Don't be afraid to test new ideas and formats based on your analytics. Experimentation can lead to discovering what truly resonates with your audience.

Example

If you notice that live cooking sessions generate high engagement, consider incorporating more live streams into your content calendar.

Seek Feedback

In addition to analyzing metrics, directly ask your audience for feedback. Use polls or community posts to gather input on what they enjoy and what they'd like to see more of.

Example

Post a question in your community tab asking, "What type of recipes do you want to see next? Let me know in the comments!" This not only engages your audience but also provides valuable insights.

Stay Flexible

The YouTube landscape is always evolving, so be prepared to adapt your strategy based on new trends and audience preferences. Staying flexible allows you to pivot when necessary.

Example
If you notice a rising trend in plant-based cooking, consider incorporating more vegan recipes into your content to capitalize on current interests.

Insights

Analyzing your growth and metrics is essential for understanding your performance on YouTube and making informed decisions to optimize your content. By monitoring key metrics such as views, watch time, audience retention, CTR, engagement, and demographics, you can gain valuable insights into what resonates with your audience. Set clear goals, evaluate content performance, and be open to experimentation and feedback. With a data-driven approach and a willingness to adapt, you'll be well-equipped to navigate your YouTube journey and continue growing your channel. So, grab your analytics toolkit and dive into the numbers—your path to success awaits!

Conclusion

Your YouTube Adventure Awaits! Congratulations, you've made it through the ultimate guide to conquering YouTube! By now, you're armed with a treasure trove of knowledge—from crafting engaging content and navigating trends to building a brand and analyzing metrics. It's like you've graduated from YouTube University, and your diploma is made of subscribers and watch time! As you embark on your YouTube journey,

Remember the key lessons

Engage Your Audience

Treat your viewers like cherished friends rather than just numbers on a screen. Respond to comments, ask questions, and create a community where everyone feels right at home—even if it's a home filled with flour dust and spilled sauce!

Stay Consistent but Evolve

Like a fine soufflé, your content needs the right balance of consistency and adaptability. Stick to a schedule, but don't be afraid to experiment—after all, who knows? Your next video could be the culinary equivalent of a viral TikTok dance!

Embrace Trends and Collaborations

Jump on trends like a cat on a laser pointer! Collaborate with other creators to expand your reach and create new, exciting content that keeps your audience coming back for more. Just remember, no one wants to see a cooking show where everyone just stares awkwardly at the camera—let's keep the energy high!

Analyze Your Growth

Use analytics like a treasure map guiding you toward your next big find. Keep an eye on what works and what doesn't, and don't hesitate to pivot. The only thing worse than a soggy bottom on a pie is sticking to a failing strategy!

Build Your Brand

Your brand is your unique flavor in the vast buffet of YouTube. Make it delicious, memorable, and distinctly yours, whether it's through a catchy tagline or a signature laugh that makes viewers feel like they're part of the family. So, go forth, brave content creator! With your newfound wisdom, sprinkle in a dash of creativity, a pinch of humor, and a generous helping of passion, and watch your channel flourish like a well-watered herb garden. Remember, the journey might be filled with challenges (and the occasional kitchen disaster), but every setback is just a chance for an epic comeback. And if all else fails, just remember: there's always room for dessert! 🎂 Here's to your YouTube success—may your views be plentiful and your comments ever positive! Now, get out there and start creating—your audience is waiting!

Good Luck

www.ingramcontent.com/pod-product-compliance
Lightning Source LLC
Chambersburg PA
CBHW070142230526
45471CB00002B/480